THE BOOK OF LOVE

KARMA AND DOPAMINE

MIKE BHANGU

BBP

ISBN: 978-1-77481-077-4 (Paperback)

Published by BB Productions
British Columbia, Canada
thinkingmanmike@gmail.com

TABLE OF CONTENTS

INTRODUCTION

Perhaps the universe coded me differently and this is why my love journey is as is. Maybe my current understanding is jaded. Perhaps I'm on the verge of enlightenment. Or maybe this is simply a confused philosopher-poet's rant.

Divided into three chapters, this short read shares my journey with love and my struggle to understand the phenomenon. Perhaps love is much more mystical than we're taught. Maybe there is more to the innate impulse constantly calling for satisfaction.

Chapter One, through poetry, shares my experience falling under the influence of popular love.

Chapter Two shares my memories of losing love, again, predominantly through poetry.

Chapter Three explores a love beyond what is popular, and hints at an unbreakable love.

CHAPTER ONE

LOVE

THE POWER OF LOVE

A mountain is a hill and an ocean a pond. My legs are those of a giant and as are my arms. A year is a day and 100 miles a few blocks. This is the power of love.

NAMELESS THING

An inch is peace. A mile is torture. Yet, there is no language that houses a sound able to describe our pull. The word "Love" doesn't suffice. The term is weak compared to this unique and nameless thing. An inch is peace. A mile is torture.

CONVERGENCE

All that is best of rainbows, sunshine, and starry nights
is found when two hearts blend, mend, and unite.

THERE IS NO BETTER EMOTION THAN THE ONE
SPUN BY THE WARMTH OF LOVE.

ENTANGLED

The flicker of love gives light during my darkest hour,
strengthens my knees, and reveals my power.
Entangled as one, the pain is replaced by peace and
tears transform into flowers.

"Love doesn't keep a score of wrongs. Love doesn't bring up past failures."

1 CORINTHIAN 13:5.

COLLISION

When we first collided, the sky kissed the mountain and the ocean parted.

CHAPTER TWO

LOST LOVE

"The false, immature lovers do not know the way of love, and so they fall."

SRI GURU GRANTH SAHIB JI, PAGE 1425.

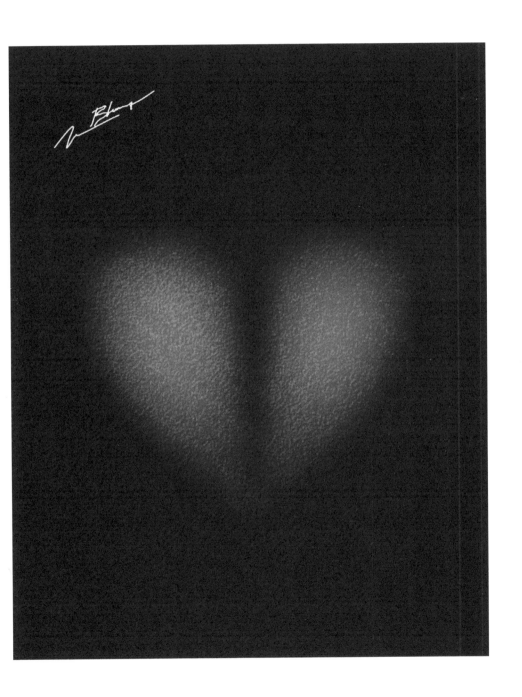

BODY CORD

The mind temporarily contorts.

The Third Eye temporarily distorts.

The soul chips at the shell.

The mouth morphs into hell.

The body reaches for its own cord,

when a lover loves no more.

LOVE LOST

Like a snowman in the summer Sun I stand.

Like a star covered by a dark blanket I am.

HUMPTY DUMPTY

I was placed on a waiting-list with over 7 billion before me. I'm begging for the world's attention so I may ask her to stop breaking me. I no longer desire to be treated as Humpty Dumpty. Rebuilding myself isn't as easy as it once be—the king's men are tired and my strength is as reliable as electricity in an Indian City. My tries at understanding love have converged into a single memory. I'm weak kneed, broken, and bleeding.

FORTY PROOF

My future looks dim, in the shadows with hope, dancing in a retro-fashioned manner, and sweating 40 proof through its pores.

REGRESSION

My eyes lost their shine.

My step forgot to stride.

My smile married a shallow grin.

Loveless I regress.

LOVE

Most commonly, "love" is a word used to describe the induced chemical relationship between people, between people and secular objects, or between people and motions as throwing the football. What I'm suggesting is that "love" is a word used to describe the cognitive inductions stimulated by a given noun or verb.

In relation, "love" is a very strong value configuration within me. It has given purpose to my existence, it has stimulated peace and belonging to surface, and it has made sense of senseless motions. Under the inductions of love, no worries enter me.

However, the loss of love can do damage and it can shock the brain into reconfiguring its chemistry and the parameters of the mind and Thought Energy. The reconfiguration can be random and irrational and the proceeding motions the same. Under the random and irrational reconfiguration, damage can be done to both the mind and one's secular existence. The experience can be similar to blowing a knee half-way through the 100-meter sprint at the Olympics.

DISCONNECTED

The modern world speaks in a foreign tongue,
and it is a language my spirit doesn't understand.

SCORNED

I'm stuck in the past while my body moves forward; time stolen from changing the world; my potential is unfulfilled.

Love can turn. A scorned lover will burn. Words can penetrate the outer armor. Unneeded drama. To challenge Karma? Can someone please kiss away this cloud-like shadow?

STUCK IN TIME

I feel as a dying star in tomorrow's sky, a grain of sand in a storm, a snowflake when it cries, and a forty-five when it's warm.

A regression is the consequence. Depression rises within. Diseased dreams surface.

Now, I'm stuck rewording past injuries; I'm stuck in one spot while the world keeps moving; I'm stuck in time and waiting for release.

RENAISSANCE ME

The renaissance me wears the heart on the sleeve and is coated by a thin skin. So, it should come as no surprise to discover that I've experienced many sad moments. I'm currently in the middle of one such occurrence.

The purpose of this article is to share a temporary remedy I reconnected with. I recently worked an upcoming Hallmark movie of the week. The character I played is a background performer and the role required that I act as a person in love.

Along with the other actors, I spent the entire day pretending to be happy and in love. Although I started the day dancing with melancholy, by nightfall my mood was bright, and during the drive home, it dawned on me. Sometimes, when depressed, simply acting the opposite can push the mind out from the darkness. It's like magic.

This is the second time I've accidentally exercised this remedy. The first came after pretending to smile and laugh for 10 hours on the set of a popular television show.

Mystically, fake smiling and laughing naturally causes happiness to invade the time and space of thought.

If I may suggest, the next time you're feeling upset, try this—meet with a friend, find a private area, and pretend. I'm serious. You'll feel better. Try it.

CHAPTER THREE

RECOVERY

PUFFED AWAY

My life as the cosmos holding a burning cigarette. She takes a heavy toke and burns me quick. Slowly in my eyes and faster as I grow, burning quicker as I shine, doesn't she know? Maybe I was wrong and this is why I'm burnt quick? I need time, please, understand, I'm learning how to love again.

ACHILLES' HEAL

Like a drug addict of a century without the drug, the withdrawal symptoms are my Achilles' Heel, and detached from love's inductions, I wasn't quick enough to dodge the arrows. In the end, I'd rather battle an ancient Viking, blindfolded, than deal with losing someone or something I love. Better yet, I'd rather love a noun or a verb that can't be lost.

SOULMATE

Movies and music have convinced almost every person that he or she is incomplete, and only another human being can complete him or her. However, a person is born whole and doesn't require another person to complete their human condition. More specifically, movies and music suggest that the soul is incomplete and it requires another soul to be whole—a soulmate. But the soul is born intact and movies and music are misleading the person.

So to further distract a person, an individual is deceived to believe that he or she must search for another to be whole. But how can a missing half to something that's complete ever be found? This deception runs deep, and for generations, the people have chased the beast.

I WAS FOOLED

Since my teens there's been an unsettling presence within me—a constant and unidentified impulse nagging at my mind's eye, like a belly nags when empty. This impulse produces feelings opposite to those of peace, purpose, and belonging.

These feelings pressured me to search for peace, purpose, and belonging, and while searching without knowing what to search for, I noticed, while under the reconfigurations of constructed love, this innate impulse and its productions seemingly silenced. In the beginning, I thought the silence meant that the innate impulse was satisfied, but after analyzing the memories, I realized that I mistakenly created associations and misidentified the inner hunger. I thought that another person, from the opposite sex, to whom I was attracted to, was what this impulse was beckoning for. However, under the blanket of constructed love, the innate impulse wasn't able to speak to the time and space of thought, and its communications were disguised.

What I thought turned to be false, and after reviewing my memories, I can't help but think that I was a fool. I fooled myself and as a consequence, every constructed love lost felt as I had died.

Constructed love references what we were taught love is by our environmental settings, and it is a value configuration. Moreover, we were trained to believe that constructed love is what the innate impulse requires before it's satisfied.

Most of the information that constitutes constructed love is learned through an individual's interactions with popular information and life experiences. This suggests that what a person believes love is, and what love should fulfill, are programmed. Hollywood is the biggest influencer and the type of love they demonstrate on the big screen is unrealistic.

So, what is this innate impulse and what is able to permanently satisfy this hunger?

REBUILT "I" BE

Rebuilt I am, back at it again, searching for dopamine. However, ambitions are different. I've learned from the cognitive reconfigurations caused by loss, that nowhere an unbreakable love be. That is, nowhere in the physical, the Universe that be visible, is there a link that will permanently satisfy me.

PLAYING DETECTIVE: MYSTICAL LOVE

My hypothesis is that nothing in the physical realm can provide a constant induction. No noun and no verb. Fortunately, only half the Universe the physical is, and now-a-days, I look to the invisible for an unbreakable stimulant.

In this quest, and after analyzing world theologies and philosophies, the mystics of our past seem to provide an explanation that I can live with and work toward.

The saints suggest that this innate impulse, the craving each living thing has, the yearning for something, a union, a completion, commonly misidentified by the contemporary person with a love for a material object or another human, is an innate desire to reunite with The Unmanifest / The Source. This is why a material object or a person cannot permanently satisfy the craving. A material object or a person only disguises the feeling, like a pharmaceutical painkiller. When the mind has grown accustom to the material object or person, the yearning will again speak to the time and space of thought. Only

The Source can provide an unbreakable and everlasting love. Only The Great Architect can satisfy the inner impulse.

To connect with The Master, suggest the mystics, a person must equally view all through the eyes of compassion, humility, truth, contentment, and unconditional love.

Love for and from The Lord is the only permanent satisfaction in the whole of existence. Endeavour I do to experience, and not just in thought but also in feeling. Thoughts and feelings are different and each is considered a unique language. To love The Lord in belief and thought is the first step. The second is to feel this love. Feelings produce vibrations and the vibration of true love resonates with the Essence of God.

> *"...This wondrous painting is now the problem. Forget this picture and focus your consciousness on the Painter. ||12||"* – (Sri Guru Granth Sahib Ji, page 340.)

I fell in love with the fruits of The Maker's labour but I forgot to love The Maker.

HAPPINESS

In my search for the state of consciousness known as happiness, I've hit many dead ends, or better put, many brick walls, and the first few I noticed only after leaving an imprint as Wiley Coyote typically does.

The brick walls I use as metaphors and to "wants" I actually refer. They were the greatest obstacles in my search for happiness and they are the cause of the sensations opposite.

A want hinders one's happiness by stimulating negative sensations. These sensations suppress the cognitive influences that produce happiness. A want can stimulate negative sensations on these occasions—when a want isn't satisfied, when the satisfaction is removed, and/or when the removal of a satisfaction is anticipated.

In accordance, it only makes sense to house fewer wants and those not easily unsatisfied. Wants constructed using such a formula are restricted in their potential to provoke negative sensations.

In my search for happiness, I've hit many dead ends, or better put, many brick walls, and I'm still occasionally leaving an imprint. Although I understand cause and effect, it's easier said than practiced. Wants are not easy to control. Nevertheless, happiness beckons I endeavour.

"And above all these put on love,
which binds everything together in perfect harmony."

COLOSSIANS 3:14.

"Do not fall in love with one who is destined to leave. O Nanak, I am a sacrifice to those who understand this."

SRI GURU GRANTH SAHIB JI, PAGE 1410.

The saints suggest that if an individual allows the soul to speak, a person will experience a love able to permanently placate.

UNCONDITIONAL LOVE

As the night embraces the stars and the rose the sun, embrace the potentials of The Father's love.

Love for another is all good so long as it doesn't morph into a prison, and trap the soul from communing with The Great Architect.

TO LOVE ANOTHER

To create a sustaining love for and from another human, in my humble opinion, a person must first genuinely love The Source. This will garner a more peaceful and harmonious relationship.

To first love The Source allows a person to selflessly, and unconditionally, love another human, and if both in the relationship love The Father, the chances of separation are greatly reduced. Moreover, if a loss of love does occur, the pain will not be as severe.

LOVE

BE LOVED

LIVE

BOOKS BY MIKE BHANGU

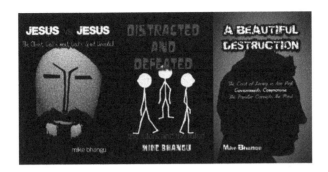

Lightning Source UK Ltd.
Milton Keynes UK
UKHW050629100621
385260UK00008B/104